THE CROSS

Stephen Kaung

ISBN: 978-1-942521-46-4

Available from:

Christian Testimony Ministry
4424 Huguenot Road
Richmond, Virginia 23235

www.christiantestimonyministry.com

Printed in USA

CONTENTS

PREFACE

The following messages on the cross were given by Stephen Kaung during July, 1988, in Santa Barbara, California. His spoken words have been transcribed into this book and edited only for clarity.

As Stephen Kaung shared, the cross is fundamental and central in the Bible, and it is very essential and vital to our lives. The cross is God's means to God's end. God's eternal purpose is His Son. He wants His Son to have the first place in all things, to sum up all things in Christ. The end is God's Son, but the cross is the only means, not just one of the means, but the only means to reach God's end.

There is a message that comes out of the cross of Christ, and it is this message that we must hear.

THE WORD OF THE CROSS

I Corinthians 1:18 For the word of the cross is to them that perish foolishness, but to us that are saved it is God's power.

The Lord has impressed upon my heart this very fundamental matter of the cross, and at the very outset, I would like to quote what some people have said on this matter. Mrs. Jessie Penn-Lewis, in her book The Centrality Of The Cross, made this point:

We need a "fixed point," which acts as a centre and a goal, and that "point" in the history of the world back to the ages before it, and forward to the ages following it is the cross of Calvary. It is the central pivot of the dealing of God with the universe in every aspect. It is because we Christians get away from the fixed point of the cross that we wander into all kinds of cul-de-sac plans where we lose the balance and right perspective of truth.

Brother T. Austin Sparks, in his book The Centrality and Universality Of The Cross, said:

The Bible when we stand back and view it as a whole gives us the views of the universe. Firstly there is the standpoint of eternity and of God's eternal purpose. From this the universe is Christo-centric. Secondly there is the standpoint (of the universe) of the incursion of sin, with all its effects. From this point of view the universe is Redempto-centric. The former represents the tremendous significance of Jesus Christ, Son of God and Son of man. The latter sets forth the terrible and glorious meaning of Jesus Christ and Him crucified; in other words, the Cross. It is with this second, as with the wheel within the greater wheel, that we are now occupied. The greater has become wholly dependent upon the other, and so the Cross becomes adorned with all the significance of the universal purpose of God from eternity to eternity.

To put it in a simple way, the cross is God's means to God's end. God's eternal purpose is His Son. He wants His Son to have the first place in all things, to sum up all things in Christ; that is,

God's end and God's means and only means to reach that end is Jesus Christ and Him crucified; that is, the cross. But the cross is not the end. Sometimes, we think of the cross as the end. No; it is not the end. The end is God's Son, Christ Jesus; but the cross is the only means not just one of the means but the only means to reach God's end. It is because of this that the cross is fundamental and central in the Bible, and it is very essential and vital to our lives.

The word of the cross is to them that perish foolishness but to us that are saved it is God's power. (I Corinthians 1:18)

The cross is not only a fact, it is also a word. We all know the historical fact of the cross that two thousand years ago our Lord Jesus was crucified and died on the cross. That is the fact. But the cross is more than just a fact; the cross is a word. There is a message coming out from that cross. The word logos means "inner thoughts" or "inner thoughts expressed," "speech," "utterance," "truth," "message." There is a message that comes out of the cross of Christ, and it is this message that we must hear.

If people approach the word of the cross by theorizing it, reasoning it, or philosophizing it, they will find that the cross, to them, is foolishness. They will reject it; and doing so, they will perish. But if we approach the word of the cross with faith and obedience, we will discover that the word of the cross is truly the power of God, and by it, we are saved. So we must approach the cross with humility, with faith, and with obedience. It is not for us to have mental exercise over it, but rather we should have that spiritual exercise as we enter into this matter of the cross. So, God willing, we look to the Lord that we will enter into the word of the cross with humility, faith, and obedience and find in it the power of God.

FOUR MESSAGES OF THE CROSS

What is the message of the cross? What does the cross speak to us? Of course, we know there are many things the cross of our Lord Jesus speaks to us; but for our time together I will limit it to just four. They are very basic in the message of the cross.

Justification

First of all, the cross speaks to us of justification. For all have sinned and come short of the glory of God (Romans 3:23). When the Holy Spirit begins to convict us of our sins, immediately, we find that we are in a state of condemnation; we have a guilty feeling. We find that there is no peace in our heart. We know that the wrath of God is upon us, and we also know that the wages of sin is death. We will cry out like the jailer in Philippi: What must I do to be saved? (Acts 16:30). And it is here that we need to hear what the cross speaks to us.

Being justified freely by his grace through the redemption which is in Christ Jesus; whom God has set forth a mercy-seat, through faith in his blood, for the shewing forth of his righteousness, in respect of the passing by the sins that had taken place before, through the forbearance of God; for the shewing forth of his righteousness in the present time, so that he should be just, and justify him that is of the faith of Jesus. (Romans 3:24- 26)

How can a man be just with God? This is an age-old question that we find being raised even in the book of Job (see Job 9:2). Job asked the question: How can a man be just with God? Humanly speaking, it is impossible. When we are convicted of our sins, we try to justify ourselves before God by doing good; but no matter how much good we do, under the light of God, our righteousnesses are as filthy rags. They just do not cover us before God. So humanly speaking, to be just with God is impossible. We have to look outside of ourselves, not from ourselves. We must look to God for justification; and thank God, He has provided. God sent His beloved Son into this world to be the Lamb of God who takes away the sin of the world. Our Lord Jesus was crucified; His blood was shed; and by the shedding of the blood, our sins are remitted.

In the Old Testament time, once a year on the Day of Atonement, the high priest would take the blood, enter behind the veil and sprinkle the blood upon the mercy seat to make atonement for the people. Because the blood was upon the mercy seat, the sin of the nation was atoned. But the reality is in our Lord Jesus, Himself, when He took His own blood and entered not into the tabernacle made of man but into heaven itself. There He made atonement for our sins. If the blood of the bulls and goats would purify people, how much more the blood of our Lord Jesus, who offered Himself spotless by the eternal Spirit, will purify us from dead works to worship the living God. In the blood of the cross of our Lord Jesus, our sins are remitted and we are justified before God, just as if we have never sinned. This is what the cross has done for us, and this is what the cross speaks to us.

We have all experienced the preciousness of the blood in forgiving our sins, cleansing us from all our unrighteousness, and making us acceptable before God that we may stand before Him with a pure conscience. The blood not only atones our sins before God but it cleanses our evil conscience and gives us peace. The blood also stops the mouth of the accuser, our enemy, so that he is no longer able to accuse us. Chapter 5 of Romans tells us that we have been washed by the blood, justified, and now we are at peace with God. We are standing in His presence, and we are in His favor. So brothers and sisters, where we are today is because of the cross. The cross has spoken, and we have believed. Because of this, we are now justified.

Separation

Secondly, the cross speaks to us of separation. Before we were saved, our most urgent problem was our sins: How can our sins be remitted? But after being saved, probably, the first problem a young believer faces is this matter of the world: How can I be separated from the world in reality? We find in Ephesians 2, before we were saved, when we were dead in sins and transgressions, we walked according to the age of this world. In other words, we belonged to this world; we were part of it. And this world attracted us. We sought after the things of this world. We wanted to be in fashion. We did not want to let people look upon us as being backward; we wanted to belong. We wanted to prove ourselves that we are fashionable. That was the situation before we were saved. But thank God, when He saved us, He not only saved us from our sins, He also saved us from this world.

When the children of Israel were in Egypt, they were in bondage. God used the Pashcal lamb to deliver them by putting the blood on the door post; and the angel of destruction passed over. They were saved from their sins and destruction through the blood of the lamb. But not only were they saved from their sins, when they were eating the lamb, they were eating in such a manner that they were ready to go out. Immediately, that night after midnight, the children of Israel began to march out of Egypt. And in order to be completely separated from Egypt, God led them in a strange way. They could have gone by the land of the Philistines into the Promised Land, the land of Canaan, but instead of doing that, God led them round about to the Red Sea. They crossed the Red Sea, and Egypt was behind them. They were separated from Egypt; and now, as the New Testament says, they belonged to Moses. In the real sense, in the New Testament, it means you belong to Christ.

Brothers and sisters, this is what baptism signifies. Some people say: "Why is it, after I am saved, I need to be baptized? Am I not saved by the blood of Jesus Christ? If I believe in the Lord

Jesus, I am saved. Why should I be baptized?" But the Lord, in typology, saved the children of Israel not only by the blood of the lamb but also by leading them through the Red Sea. They were saved not only from destruction but from Egypt. They were set apart for Moses, that is, for God.

What is baptism? Why should we be baptized? You remember on the day of Pentecost, after Peter spoke, the people were pricked in heart and they said, "What should we do?" Then Peter said: "Repent, and be baptized. Be saved from this perverse generation." So baptism actually signifies that we are saved from this world. Formerly, we belonged to this world; but through baptism, through the water, we are saved from this world, and now we belong to another One or to a new world. We belong to Christ; He is now our world. That is what baptism signifies.

Have we been baptized? We have. Do we know what it means? Are we being separated from the world? God has separated us, but how much is this separation a reality in our lives? As a new believer, you do not really need somebody to tell you what the world is; and if anybody should tell you, probably that is not it. But after you are saved, with the life of Christ within you and what the cross has already done for you, invariably, the Holy Spirit will begin to speak to you of what the cross has done for you in relation to the world. In the beginning it will be the things of the world because, formerly, this is what we loved. They were life to us. But after we are saved the Spirit of God will begin to convict us of the things of this world, the lust of the eyes, the lust of the flesh, the pride of life, things that we loved to see. But we begin to realize that this is not convenient, not right for God's people. Or maybe they are things we love to have but now begin to realize these are the things we should let go of. Brothers and sisters, God, by His Holy Spirit, will begin to deal with us concerning the world because we have already been separated. The cross stands between us and the world, and the Holy Spirit is now to make this a reality to us. So, one by one, gradually, you have to let go of this thing or you have to let go of the other thing.

For young Christians, probably, in the beginning, there will be some struggle. I will just use this as an illustration. When I was first saved, the Lord began to deal with me especially in this matter of theater, cinema, movies because before I was saved, that was the thing I liked. When I opened the newspaper, that was the first thing I looked for. At that time, I was in Shanghai where there were many cinemas, and I had relatives and friends who owned theaters so I didn't have to pay anything. But after I was saved, the Lord began to deal with me on this matter. Oh, how I struggled over it and how I reasoned with the Lord and said, "Now I will just go to see the good movies; I will stop all the bad movies." So I struggled over this matter, and then I told the Lord I would just go to see religious movies. Sure enough, the last movie I went to the theater to see was a religious movie. Somebody sent us tickets, and I struggled within myself: "It is a pity to give that up. It is a religious movie. Of course I can go." So I went; and I have to testify that during those two hours in the theater, I was looking at the movie, and yet I was not seeing it. Why? Because there was such a struggle within me, and it was not a good one either. So when I walked out of the theater, that was the last one I was in, by the grace of

14

God. Brothers and sisters, maybe, in the beginning it was quite a struggle; but later on, I found that what I gave up was nothing to compare with what the Lord has given to me. It is really not a loss; it is a gain.

Afterwards, my relatives, seeing that I didn't go to the movies anymore, pitied me. I remember my aunt told me: "It is a pity. You are a young man and you should go and enjoy yourself. If you need money, I will give it to you so that you can go and enjoy yourself." In China, we dare not talk against older people, but I laughed in my heart. I said: "You don't know. I don't need it. I have something far better. It is a joy; it is such a peace in my heart. It is not difficult." But in the beginning, probably, it will be difficult.

God will deal with you on this matter of separation. As you begin to draw closer to the Lord, as you begin to grow in the Lord, it is not because you let go of a few things in this world, therefore, you are separated. You begin to find that the world is in you. There is that spirit of the world in us, and how it takes hold of us! We not only need deliverance from these things, we need to be delivered from the very spirit of the world.

The world is a system, a cosmos. Satan organized the world into a very tight system, and it includes all areas and aspects of things, political, economic, cultural, social, and even religious. After we are saved, the Lord will not only deliver us from the things of the world but He will deliver us from the very spirit of the world; and the strongest spirit of the world is found in the religious world.

Paul was deeply in the religious world of Judaism. In Philippians 2, he tells us how he was deeply rooted in Judaism: he was circumcised on the eighth day; he was born an Israelite; he was of the tribe of Benjamin; he was the son of a Pharisee; according to the letter of the law, he was perfect; he was above his contemporaries in zeal for God; and he was persecuting the Christians, thinking that they were the impostors, the rebels. He was deeply rooted in that religious world; and yet, God delivered him from the very spirit of it. He said: I count all these things to be loss (Philippians 3:8). These things were precious to him, these things were his achievement, these were the things that he was proud of; and now, he considered these things as dross, as refuse, as things to be despised because of the excellency of the knowledge of Jesus Christ. That man was completely delivered from the religious world into the fulness of Christ.

Have we been delivered from the world? Have we been delivered from the spirit of the world? Have we been delivered from the world as a system? Do we enter into the fulness of Christ, knowing that the excellency of the knowledge of Christ is a gain? As you go on with the Lord, you are continuously being separated from the world, and it is just a confirmation of what the cross has already done for you. Positionally, we have the cross standing between us and the world. Experientially, we find that sometimes when the world looks at us, it still has hope in us; and when we look at the world, we still have some desire for it. We are not dead to each other.

But far be it for me to boast save in the cross of our Lord Jesus Christ, through whom the world is crucified to me, and I to the world. (Galatians 6:14)

Paul said when he looked at the world, he saw that the world was dead. It was crucified; it was dead. There was nothing that he admired. And at the same time, when the world looked at him, it found that he was dead. In other words, it had given up hope on him.

I wonder if the world has really given up hope on us, or whether the world is still trying to tempt us, to draw us back because it finds there is still something of its spirit within us. Do we really look at the world as dead? Can we boast in this way? What we need is to return to the cross. If we look to the cross, there will be a revelation given to us. You know, the cross is a great revelation. It not only reveals the love of God and the sinfulness of sins, it also reveals to us the ugliness, the hostility of the world because it is the world that crucified our Lord Jesus. The world cries out: "Away with Him, away with Him. Crucify Him." The world rejected Him. That is what the world did or is doing to our Lord Jesus. Now if we know the cross, if we see the cross, and if we see it is the world that crucified Christ, brothers and sisters, where are we? Can we love the world anymore? And will the world love us anymore if we really stand with Christ on the cross?

Deliverance

Thirdly, the cross speaks to us of deliverance. When you begin to grow more in the Lord and you have some dealings with the world too, then you find there is something within you that troubles you. When we were saved, we heard the Lord say to us, "Your sins are forgiven; go and sin no more." I think every believer has heard that. If you are really saved, you know that the Lord has spoken to you saying that your sins are forgiven; but more, He said, "Go and sin no more." Deep down within us, we know that we should not sin anymore because it is our sins that nailed Christ to the cross, and how can we sin anymore? We do not want to sin anymore, and we try not to sin. But after the first excitement of salvation begins to subside, we find that what we do not want to do, we do; and what we hate, we do; what we love to do, we cannot. In our spirit, we want to please God, we want to do the will of God; and yet we find that in our flesh, there is no good. So far as our will is concerned, we will to do God's will; and yet in the members of our body there seems to be another law there. That law of sin and death is so powerful that our will is no match to that law. As we begin to grow in the Lord, the more we want to please God, the more we find that we are unable to. We find the more we want to do the will of God, the more we are not able to do it. On the contrary, we are doing things we know we should not do and we do not want to do.

Before we were saved, when we did the things we liked to do, we were happy; we felt fulfilled. There was the pleasure of sin there. But after we are saved, when we fall into the same thing, are we happy about it? We find that it is painful. We find that we do not like to do it. We find that it is horrible; it is defiled.

Dear brothers and sisters, is it not true that sin is not only an act, it is a principle? There is sin that dwells in us, in our flesh, and it rules and reigns over us. We are helpless. No matter how strong our will is, it cannot withstand a law. The law is always stronger than the will; and we will cry out like Paul in chapter 7 of Romans: Oh, wretched man that I am! Who shall deliver me out of this body of death? (v.24). Is this not our cry? We want to be delivered from this principle of sin, from this power of sin; and how we struggle! Sometimes, we seem to be able to overcome; but more often, we are defeated. Our life is just up and down, up and down; and we know that this is not the life that God wants us to live. But how?

One day, the Holy Spirit leads us back to the cross, and the cross begins to speak to us.

What then shall we say? Shall we continue in sin that grace may abound? Far be the thought. We who have died to sin, how shall we still live in it? Are you ignorant that we, as many as have been baptised unto Christ Jesus, have been baptised unto his death? We have been buried therefore with him by baptism unto death, in order that, even as Christ has been raised up from among the dead by the glory of the Father, so we also should walk in newness of life. For if we are become identified with him in the likeness of his death, so also we shall be of his resurrection; knowing this, that our old man has been crucified with him, that the body of sin might be annulled, that we should no longer serve sin. (Romans 6:1-6)

We are led back to the cross. Are you ignorant? Do you not know? Have you not been baptized? And the very baptism tells you that you are dead with Christ. You were buried with Christ, and you are now risen with Christ so that you may walk in newness of life. By death, you have died to sin, and by living, you are alive to God. Don't you know that? In other words, the Holy Spirit will lead you back to the cross. There is no way of deliverance other than the cross. We may try to deliver ourselves from the power of sin, just as we tried before to deliver ourselves from committing many sins. We cannot do that; it is the cross.

There on the cross, our Lord Jesus died, not only as our substitute but also as our representative. He not only died for us, He also died as us. In other words, when Christ died on the cross, He took the whole Adamic race, the old man, with Him; and when He died, that old man died with Him and in Him. To put it more personally, when Christ died on the cross, He bore our sins in His body, your sins, my sins, and there He suffered the penalty of it. He died; He shed His blood for the remission of my sins. Thank God for that, that is a fact; and I believe in that fact. My sins are forgiven. But the cross is more than that: Christ also died on the cross as us, not only for us but as us. He not only bore our sins, He bore us. He took you and me, the old man, the Adamic race. He took all of us into Him. And when He died, the Adamic race was finished. The old man is dead; you and I have died in Him. That is the fact of the cross, and it was done two thousand years ago. You do not need to crucify yourself. You cannot crucify yourself, and you do not need to because, two thousand years ago God did it for you in Christ Jesus. God knows that there is no good in you nor in me, that we are beyond repair, beyond improvement. If we could be improved, God would do it. But God has already seen that we are beyond repair, beyond improvement; and God said, Finish with it. So when Christ died on the cross, He finished the old creation in Christ; and He said, It is finished. You and I were finished there on the cross. God has done it in Christ Jesus. It is a fact, and all we need to do is to believe that fact.

Sometimes, believers find this very difficult; just like before we were saved, it was very difficult to believe how Christ could die for us. How can His blood cleanse our sins? He died two thousand years ago, and I am sinning today. How could He die for us two thousand years ago? It was very difficult; because if you try to reason it out, it is foolishness, and you will perish. But when the word of the cross is spoken to your heart by the Holy Spirit, you just believe it. You accept that fact and say, "Thank God, it is so"; and it is so. You experienced the power of God in forgiving your sins, and since you have that experience already, it should be easier, not harder. Now the same thing is true with our being dead in Him. If you are still struggling with sin, with the power of sin, with temptations and all these things, stop struggling; just believe. Rest in the fact that when Christ died, you died.

Our old man was crucified: Knowing this, that our old man has been crucified with him... (Romans 6:6).

It is not that our old man is crucified now or shall be crucified, but it was crucified two thousand years ago. It must be dead, very dead. Now do you accept that fact? If you accept that fact, you experience the power of God in deliverance because the Bible says our old man has been crucified with Him that the body of sin might be annulled that we should no longer serve sin.

Sin as a principle reigns in our flesh. Sin is the master over the old man. The old man belongs to sin because Adam surrendered to it in the garden of Eden. Sin is the master, the old man is the steward, and the body is the servant. Sin as the master cannot give orders to the body directly. It has to go through the steward, and the steward relates that order to the body to commit sin. What God did was to isolate it, but sin is still there. Brothers and sisters, God does not take away sin from you. As long as you live, sin as a principle still dwells there. The power of sin is there; it does not die. But you die. How are we delivered from sin? Not by overcoming it, but by dying to it. It is not that the root of sin is eradicated so there is no more sin. No; sin is still there. But God did such a marvelous work of isolating it because the old man is in between and is dead. So when sin tries to give the orders, nobody will take them. The body is unemployed and has nothing to do. Our body was the body of sin. That was the job the body was doing. But now the body is out of a job; it has nothing to do. That is the reason why the Bible says yield the members of your body to righteousness, unto holiness (see Romans 6:13). It is reemployed, under new management.

This is how it is. Just accept the fact; just look at the cross. If you look at the cross, it will speak to you; and the word is: You are dead. The power then becomes a reality in your life, and you are delivered from sin. This is deliverance. It is the cross. The cross speaks to us, and we are delivered. So we need to continually, steadfastly stand on the ground of the cross; and by standing on the ground of the cross, we find sin has no power over us. We are not under sin but under the grace of God.

Victory

Fourthly, the cross speaks to us of victory. As we go on with the Lord, as we know something of the forgiveness of sin, something of being separated from the world and we begin to experience the deliverance from the power of sin, then we are faced with a spiritual warfare. There is an invisible world just as real as the visible world. As a matter of fact, the invisible world is even more real than the visible world because the visible world is appearance, but the invisible world is the reality. Oftentimes, after you have gone on with the Lord, you begin to realize there is a spiritual world there; an invisible world is opened to you, and you are faced with enemies. It is just like in the Promised Land, there were giants, there were enemies. We are not wrestling against flesh and blood; we are wrestling against principalities, authorities, powers of darkness, and evil spirits reigning in the heavenlies. That is what our battle is.

Oftentimes, the enemy will use things, environment, or even people. They are the agents, as it were, of the enemy; but the enemy is actually behind it. Now if our attention is focused upon people, we are fighting the wrong battle. If our focus is upon our environment or upon things or events, then we are deceived. That is the reason why, so often, we get into all kinds of problems and troubles because our eyes are upon persons, things, or environment. These are not real, but behind it there is the enemy; and he is out to kill, to murder, to deceive, to attack, to tempt, and to accuse because he is the accuser of the brethren. He is a liar; he is a murderer from the very beginning; and he is the great deceiver, the tempter.

The enemy is there, and he is using all kinds of means and ways and vows, trying to cheat us, trying to deceive us, trying to defeat us, trying to kill us. Unfortunately, we do not realize it. We look at what is visible. We think that a certain brother or sister is after us. We think that our environment is just too bad, and we need to change it, then it will be all right. We just try to get away from this or from that, and we try to fight against these things. We are in the wrong battle. We need to realize that the enemy is behind it; and his purpose is to frustrate God's purpose in our lives, to hinder us from entering into the fulness of Christ to possess our possessions. Now that is what he is trying to do.

Another thing we need to remember is that from the human standpoint, our enemy is more intelligent than we are. He is more powerful than we are because he is a spirit. We are no match for him. If we try to fight against our enemy Satan, the adversary, by ourselves, then we will be defeated. But thank God for the message of the cross. Before our Lord Jesus went to the cross, He said: Now is the judgment of this world; now shall the prince of this world be cast out (John 12:31). On the cross, He not only shed His blood for the remission of our sins, He was not only crucified as us to deliver us from the power of sin, but He defeated the archangel, the enemy. He spoiled the principalities and authorities, He made a show of them publicly, and He put them to shame by the cross (see Colossians 2:15). In other words, on the cross our Lord Jesus has overcome the enemy. He has disarmed the strong man; He has bound the strong man; He has cast out the strong man; He has put the strong man under His feet. And that victory is decisive; that victory is full and final.

Brothers and sisters, all we need to do is look at the cross of Calvary. All we need to do is stand on that higher ground of victory. All we need to do is proclaim the victory over people, over environment, over events, and over things. And we will find it is in Christ Jesus, by His cross, that we gain the victory over the enemy. We are not dealing with an enemy that has a higher ground over us. Actually, we are dealing with an enemy below us. He is a defeated foe; and all we need to do is claim the victory of Christ. When he tries to accuse us, we avail ourselves of the blood of the Lamb, and his mouth is shut. When he tries to attack us, we flee to Calvary to the cross, to the city of refuge, and we are protected. When he tries to oppress us, we claim the victory of Christ, and our spirit is lifted. When you are in a situation where the enemy is trying to press you down, claim the victory of Christ and the air will be cleared and you will be in that ascended position. It is the message of the cross. Do not try to fight the enemy on your own. It is foolishness. But when you are faced with the enemy, confront him with the cross of Christ, and there is the victory.

This is the word of the cross. The cross is a fact, and that fact speaks to us of justification, of separation, of deliverance, and of victory. How much have we heard? He that has an ear, let him hear what the Spirit says to the churches. Let us hear the voice that comes out from the cross of our Lord Jesus. Thank God for the cross of Christ.

Shall we pray:

Dear Heavenly Father, how we do praise and thank Thee that the cross is an eternal fact. It never changes. We praise and thank Thee that what the cross has accomplished is eternal, unalterable, and permanent. We just pray that the cross may speak to each one of us. If we need justification, Lord, speak to us by the cross. If we need separation, speak to us by it. If we need deliverance, speak to us by it; and if we need victory, speak to us by it. Oh Lord, we just pray that Thou will enable us to go back to the cross and find there our Lord Jesus. In the name of our Lord Jesus. Amen.

THE WAY OF THE CROSS

John 12:24-26 Verily, verily, I say unto you, Except the grain of wheat falling into the ground die, it abides alone; but if it die, it bears much fruit. He that loves his life shall lose it, and he that hates his life in this world shall keep it to life eternal. If any one serve me, let him follow me; and where I am, there also shall be my servant. And if any one serve me, him shall the Father honour.

Shall we pray:

Dear Heavenly Father, our hearts do go out to Thee in worship and in praise. We do praise and thank Thee for knowing that Thou are here with us. We are in Thy presence; and we do trust Thy Holy Spirit to quicken Thy Word to our hearts that, truly, it may be life and spirit to us, to the praise of Thy glory. We do commit this time into Thy hands, and we trust Thee to do the work that Thou does desire to do in each one of us. In the name of our Lord Jesus. Amen.

The cross is not only an act, something that happened in history once and forever, but the cross is also a way. It is a way that we have to walk throughout our lives. The cross is not only a door to life, it is also the way of life. It is a historical fact that two thousand years ago, once and forever, our Lord Jesus went to the cross. But we also know from the Word of God that our Lord Jesus actually is a Lamb slain from the foundation of the world. Even though that act of crucifixion happened only at a certain point of time, yet so far as the Lord is concerned, He has been walking in the way of the cross even from the foundation of the world.

In order to know the way of the cross, first of all, we need to know what the meaning of the cross is. What is the ultimate meaning of the cross? What really is the cross? Paul said: We preach not of ourselves, but we preach Jesus Christ and Him crucified (see I Corinthians 1:23). There are two aspects to the center of the universe. One aspect is viewed from the eternal purpose of God; and that is, the center of the universe is none other than Jesus Christ, the Person of our Lord Jesus, the Son of God, the Son of Man. Then there is another aspect of this center. It is from the viewpoint of redemption, and that center is Him crucified, the cross. The cross is Him crucified. In other words, the cross is not something outside of you, detached from you that is put to death. The cross is where the person himself is put to death. Satan made a very clear observation when he said: Skin for skin; a man is willing to give up everything for his life (see Job 2:4). And how true it is. We are willing to give up everything but ourselves. We want to save ourselves to the extent that we are willing to let everything go if we can keep ourselves, and this is where the offense of the cross is. Why is it that people are offended by the cross? It is because it demands our very life. It is a terrible thing, and that is the reason why the cross is something we naturally will try to avoid.

THE LAMB SLAIN

Our Lord Jesus had walked in the way of the cross even from the foundation of the world. He was the Lamb slain from the foundation of the world (see Revelation 13:8). I think, probably, we need to make a distinction. He is not the

Lamb slain before the foundation of the world as we sometimes sing in our chorus. Actually, the Scripture never puts it that way. He is the Lamb slain from the foundation of the world because before the foundation of the world, there is the eternal purpose of God, and it is the Son that is in view. "From the foundation of the world" is related to God's counsel or His plan. God, seeing that the man whom He created would fall, made provision even before He created man. From the foundation of the world, He had already made the provision, and the provision was the Lamb. So the Lamb was slain from the foundation of the world, not before the foundation of the world.

THE CROSS DEMONSTRATED IN INCARNATION

He Emptied Himself

In the fulness of time, God sent His Son into this world. And this matter of incarnation is a tremendous step of the Lord Jesus, the Son of God, taking the way of the cross. In Philippians 2, it says, He who is equal with God, that is, the Son of God. He is equal with God; and this was not something that He had to grasp at because that is what He is. It is His. He is one with the Father from eternity. Yet He emptied Himself, taking up the form of a bondslave, taking upon Himself the likeness of a man. Think of that: He, being God, in the form of God, emptied Himself. Form there means "the inward reality." He has the inward reality of God because He is God; and, as God, He has everything for Himself. But because of His love for us, He emptied Himself. Of course, He cannot empty Himself of His deity; that is impossible. Even when He was on earth as man, He was still God. But He emptied Himself of all the glory and honor and majesty that surrounded Him as God. He denied Himself of all these things.

He Denied Himself

Does God need to deny Himself? Can God deny Himself? In one sense, He cannot because in II Timothy, it is said: If we are unfaithful, He abides faithful, for He cannot deny Himself (2:13). God, being God, is always faithful to Himself. So in one sense, He cannot deny Himself. But in another sense, because of His love for us, He was willing to lay aside and give up the rights that are rightly His as God. He was willing to let all these things go, and that was denying Himself.

He Took The Form Of A Bondslave

God, being God, is sovereign. He has every right. We have no right to question Him. He does not need to answer to anybody because He is God; but here you find our Lord Jesus emptied Himself. He gave up every right that belonged to Him and took up the form of a bondslave. However humble we are as human beings, we have some rights; and how often we stand on our rights. But a slave is a person who has absolutely no right. He has no right even to life. Think of that: The Son of God, who has every right, gave up His right as God and became a bondslave in reality with no right whatsoever, no right even to His own life. What an emptying! This is the way of the cross demonstrated in incarnation.

THE PERFECT MAN

The Word of God tells us how He, being in the likeness of man, lived upon this earth. The Gospel according to John tells us again and again of this Man. For instance, in John 5, the Lord Jesus said: Verily, verily I say unto you, I can do nothing of myself. What I do is because I have seen the Father doing it (v.19). And again, He said: I do not judge according to My own will, I judge according to what I hear; and My judgement is true because I do not seek My own will but the will of Him who sent Me (v.30). In John 7, He said: Your time is always ready, but My time is not yet come (v.8). John 8: I cannot say anything out of Myself; I speak because I have heard My Father saying it (v.28). Here is a Man; He denied Himself to the uttermost. Surely He could have done lots of things as a human being, especially Him who was a perfect Man. Surely He could have said many things, much more than we can say; but He denied Himself. He said: I can say nothing; I can do nothing. Whatever I say, it is what I have heard. Whatever I do, it is what My Father is doing.

He Overcame Temptation

Do you think that, being a perfect Man, our Lord Jesus was not tempted at all? Surely, as a Man, He was tempted; and the Scripture does say He was tempted in all things, but without sin (see Hebrews 4:15). Every temptation that a human being can go through, our Lord Jesus was tempted by. He learned obedience by the things which He suffered (Hebrews 5:8). Sometimes, we think that our Lord Jesus, even though He was a Man, and such a perfect Man, that surely, He never went through the things that we are going through. But that is not true. When our Lord Jesus was on this earth, He was a perfect Man; and being a Man, He was tempted in all things, much more than we are.

Before He came out to minister, after His baptism, He was led by the Spirit into the wilderness, and there He was tempted by the devil; and how He was tempted. In the three temptations that are recorded, He was tempted as a Man physically, mentally and spiritually. Physically, He was hungry after forty days and nights of fasting; and naturally, He felt hungry. So the tempter came to Him and said, "Now You, being the Son of God, can turn the stone into bread and satisfy Your hunger." But our Lord Jesus denied Himself. Then Satan led Him to a high place, the pinnacle of the temple, and said:

"If You jump down, then everybody will know that You came from heaven. You do not need to go through the cross, and You can be crowned." But our Lord Jesus denied Himself. Again, He was taken to a high mountain and shown all the riches of the world; and Satan said, 'If You bow to me, all these I will give to You." The Lord said: "Satan, get away. Worship the Lord Thy God alone" (see Matthew 4:1-11). He was tempted physically, mentally, and spiritually; but He overcame.

He Denied Himself Emotionally

As you read the gospels, you find that throughout His life, as a Man, He denied Himself all the time. He took up the cross in His emotional life. Even though the crucifixion happened at the last, the shadow the cross cast was very long. Throughout His earthly life, He took the way of the cross; and emotionally, He denied Himself. When His mother, expecting Him to do a miracle, said, "There is no more wine," our Lord Jesus said, "Woman, My time has not yet come" (see John 2:5). When He was busily serving, His family was standing outside; and the word came to Him that His family wanted to see Him. What did the Lord Jesus say? He looked around and said: "Who are My mother, brothers and sisters? Those who do the will of God" (see Matthew 12:46-50). Even His brothers in the flesh did not believe Him and said: "Do not hide yourself in this hilly place. Go to Jerusalem at the time of Feast to show yourself to the people." But the Lord said, "My time is not yet come" (see John 7:1-8). Emotionally, our Lord Jesus always denied Himself.

He Denied Himself Mentally

Mentally, it was the same thing. After the people received the five loaves and two fishes and were satisfied, they wanted to make Him King. What a temptation that must have been! Even His disciples wanted our Lord Jesus to be King, and He had to send them away. Then He dispersed the crowd and went to the mountain and prayed. Brothers and sisters, there must have been a tremendous mental struggle there. Think of that: As a human being you have the opportunity to be king, and you turn it away.

Our Lord Jesus said something that was very difficult when He said: "If you drink My blood and eat My flesh, you have eternal life in you; and in the last days I will raise you from the dead. I am the bread from heaven" (see John 6:53-58). When all the people who had been fed before and were following Him heard this word, they said it was too hard. Not only did the crowd leave Him, but many of His disciples left Him. The Lord turned to the twelve and said: "Do you want to go too? If you want to, you may" (see John 6:67). What a denying in the mental realm!

The life of our Lord Jesus with His disciples was a very difficult one. Many times He tried to tell something to His disciples, and they did not hear it; they misunderstood Him completely. That must have been a tremendous limitation to our Lord Jesus. How He must have felt straitened because His disciples could not understand Him. Now brothers and sisters, you want people to understand you. If you try and try and they misunderstand you, what do you think? Do you feel frustrated to the point of withdrawing yourself? But our Lord Jesus was with the twelve for three years, and even to the very last, they did not understand Him. How patient He was with them. How He must have suffered mentally.

He Denied His Will

In chapter 12 of the Gospel According to John, we find some Greeks wanted to see Him. Humanly speaking, we would say not only the Jews but now the Greeks wanted to see Him. This must have been His most glorious time. Yet the Lord Jesus said: Verily, verily, I say unto you, except the grain of wheat falling into the ground dies, it abides alone; but if it die it bears much fruit (John 12:24). Then He was very sorrowful in His soul, and He said: Father, if it be possible, let this time be passed from Me; but I came for this time. Father, glorify Thy name (John 12:27).

Then He entered into the garden of Gethsemane with the eleven disciples. He left eight behind and took three with Him, and He asked them to watch with Him for a moment. The Scripture says that He was very sorrowful in His soul. He was depressed. You may think that the Lord never entered into depression, but the Bible says He was very sorrowful and was depressed. He went forward and said: My Father, if it be possible, let this cup pass from me; but not as I will, but as thou wilt (Matthew 26:39). He denied His will in order to do the will of the Father.

THE CALL TO FOLLOW HIM

Throughout the life of our Lord Jesus, He denied Himself, walking the way of the cross, and this ended up at Calvary. There He was crucified, and He died for us. Now He is calling us to follow Him. He had traveled the way of the cross until, finally, He was crucified there. Now He is calling us to follow Him. The difference is that He walked the way of the cross and ended on Calvary's cross; but we begin with the cross of Christ, and then travel the way of the cross.

Brothers and sisters, we will never be able to travel the way of the cross unless, first of all, we see what the cross of Christ is. Without knowing the meaning of the cross of our Lord Jesus, without receiving the message of the cross of Christ, we will not have the incentive nor the power to walk in the way of the cross. It is impossible. So we have to start our life with the cross of our Lord Jesus. There we know our sins are forgiven; there we are separated from the world; there we are delivered from the power of sin; there we see the victory of Christ over all the powers of darkness. And only after we have received the cross of Christ into our life do we find, on the one hand, we will be constrained by the love of Christ, and on the other hand, we will be strengthened by the power of the Holy Spirit. Only then are we able to walk the way of the cross.

For the love of the Christ constrains us, having judged this: that one died for all, then all have died; and he died for all, that they who live should no longer live to themselves, but to him who died for them and has been raised. (II Corinthians 5:14-15)

We will begin with the cross of Christ, constrained by His love, empowered by His strength, and there we will take up our cross and follow the Lord. I remember Dr. Andrew Murray once said, "The cross of Christ bears us that we may bear our cross." In other words, the power of bearing our cross to follow the Lord comes from the cross of our Lord Jesus.

THE CENTRAL MEANING OF THE CROSS

I Must Be Crucified

I would like to read something written by Jessie Penn-Lewis because I feel she puts it in such a beautiful and clear way that I could not do.

We have spoken of the Cross and death to sin, as shown in Romans 6; the Cross and death to the world as in Galatians 6; and sometimes of the "grain of wheat" death-life depicted in John 12:24, but we may get light about all these aspects of the Cross and experience a measure of deliverance through the truth, and yet not know deep, deep down in our innermost being, this change of the I centre which the apostle speaks about in II Corinthians 5:14. To put it in other words, there is something needing dealing with deeper than "sin" or "the world." It is the selfhood, "the ego," the I. Has the Cross penetrated there? It is this bedrock basis of the inner life which we must get down to and examine in the light of the Cross. No other way can the Lord set free in us His rivers of living water, nor can we be brought into the place of authority over the power of darkness, for the selfhood is poisoned at its source by the fallen nature of the first Adam.

Brothers and sisters, this is the very central meaning of the cross. Now it is true, on the cross, our Lord Jesus has born our sins and taken them away. It is true that, on the cross, our old man was crucified, and we were delivered from the power of sin within us. It is also true that, by the cross, we were separated from the world. The world will look at us as dead, and we look at the world as dead; that is true. But it is the I, the person, that you must abhor. It is not something outside of you. It is your very life, your very self. I must be crucified on the cross. Otherwise, you do not know what the cross is.

The Lord illustrated this with a grain of wheat. We know that He meant to apply that parable to Himself, in the first place, because He is that grain of wheat falling into the ground and dying. But the principle applies to all of us. God often uses natural things, things on this earth to illustrate to us heavenly things because the principles are the same. He said, "A grain of wheat..." When you look at the grain of wheat, you find it may have a very beautiful shell, but that shell is hard. The life of the wheat is locked up in that shell, and even if you put it on the desk and leave it for one hundred years, it will still be there. The life in that shell is still living, but there is only that one grain of wheat there. In order to reproduce or multiply, that grain of wheat must fall from the ear of the wheat into the ground and be buried in darkness. The outer shell will deteriorate; it is destroyed. But life begins to shoot up from the earth, and it bears one hundredfold, sixtyfold and thirtyfold of fruits.

Now of course, this refers to our Lord Jesus, Himself, because before we were saved, we were all tares, weeds. We were nothing. We had appearance like wheat, eatable, but actually, we were but weeds. But thank God, Christ Jesus is the first grain of wheat. He fell from heaven to earth and from earth to under. He died, was buried, but He was resurrected; and in resurrection, He gave His life to many of us. Today, we have that wheat life within us. We have eternal life in us. We have the life of the

Spirit in us. We have God's life in us. We have Christ in us. Within us, there is life, the wheat life, the Christ life, the spiritual life. It is in us, in our spirit; but outside of that life is the shell.

The Soul Life

What is that shell? That shell is our soul. As the spirit is in the soul, so the spirit life is enclosed by the soul life. Within us there is the spirit life, Christ life, eternal life, abundant life, fulness of life; but it is being locked up by our soul life. As long as it is locked up by our soul life, this spirit life has no chance to burst forth into many grains. One thing we need to remember: It is not the soul that dies; it is the soul life that dies. Sometimes, people think that we need to let the soul die; but the soul is an organ created by God, and it is a most important part of man because man is called a soul. Soul gives us our personality. We can think, we can feel, we can decide on things, we can reason, we can make decisions, and we can choose. This represents our personality. In other words, the soul is the person. It is not the soul that needs to be destroyed; it is not the soul that needs to be crucified and done away with so that you become a soulless person. This is not God's will. It is the soul life that dies.

What is the soul life? The soul life is the self, I, that fallen nature. The Lord Jesus said, "He who loves his life shall lose it, but he who loses his life for My sake shall gain it to eternity" (see Luke 9:24). The word life there is the same word as the soul. It is the soul life, self, I, the fallen man, me, the ego, the selfhood. If you love your soul life, you will lose it. If you try to satisfy or fulfill your soul life, your I, your self, then you will lose it. But if you are willing to lose it, as if unfulfilled, for the sake of Christ, you will gain it to eternity.

If anyone serve me, let him follow me (John 12:26). He is calling us to walk the way of the cross. It is not a matter of being delivered from the power of sin; it is not a matter of just overcoming temptations that come from outside; it is the dying to ourselves. We may have experienced forgiveness; we may have experienced separation; even deliverance, to a certain degree; or victory, sometimes. But unless this self is put to death, the life of Christ has no way to flow as rivers of living water. It is not a matter of being dead to sin; it is a matter of being dead to self.

How much has the cross really worked in our lives? Brothers and sisters, our problem, our rock bottom problem is here, not only individually, but corporately. One day, we, like Job, must say we abhor ourselves. Job was a perfect man. Even God could challenge Satan with Job and said: Have you noticed, observed Job? (Job 1:8). Certainly, Satan did. He was a perfect man, upright; and yet, the I there was so strong. He was self-righteous, and this self-righteousness was so strong in him. All his things could be taken away; all his children could be taken away; his wife could not tempt him; nor could his friends argue with him and defeat him. Job was a person who was so perfect, so strong, so self-righteous; but it was I. Then God revealed Himself to Job, and he said: "I heard of You before, but now I see You. I repent in dust and ashes; I abhor myself" (see Job 42:5-6).

Brothers and sisters, if you have a beautiful I, a righteous I, will you not boast of yourself? Do you not think that this is what life is? But if it is not the life of Christ, it is you; this has to go to death. Otherwise, there is no hope. We need a revelation from God, a revelation of myself. We need such a revelation that when we look at ourselves, we are afraid of ourselves; we abhor ourselves; we hate ourselves. And it is only under such light that we are willing to die daily. As Paul said, "That we may bear in our body the dying of Jesus that the life of Jesus may be upon other people." This is the cross.

The basic problem with believers today, especially with believers who are really seeking the Lord, is this matter of the selfhood, that righteous, perfect, good selfhood. That is the hard shell. You have never been broken. There are no cracks, no wounds, no scars. You are so perfect that even God cannot reach you. There may be the life of God in you, but it is locked up. How we need the cross working in our lives. This soul life must be lost for the sake of Christ.

THE SOUL LIFE MUST BE DEALT WITH

Some people are strong in the emotional side of their soul life. With others it is in the intellectual side, and with some people their soul life may be very strong in the volitional side. Everybody is different. The combinations are all different. Now if you are strong in the emotional life, that is where God will deal with you very drastically; if you are strong in the intellectual side, that is where the Lord will deal with you especially; and if you are strong in the volitional side, that is where you need to be dealt with, until that self is put to death; until it is no longer I, it is Christ who lives in me.

Emotional Life

In Matthew 10, the Lord Jesus said: If you love your father and mother more than Me, you cannot be My disciple; if you love your brother and sister and even your own life, more than Me, you cannot be My disciple; if you love your life, you will lose it; if you lose it for My sake, you will gain it for eternity (vv.37-39). The love for our father and mother, our brother and sister, our children, our wife or husband, our own life that is natural. In Romans, chapter 1, one of the sins listed there is "without natural affection." That is a sin. If you do not love your father and mother or your brother and sister, that is a sin. That is natural affection. But here it has nothing to do with the matter of sin, it is dealing with that which is natural. The Lord said, "If you love your mother and father more than Me, you cannot be My disciple." Our emotional life needs to be dealt with. When you love those who are near to you, close to you, you get a satisfaction in your soul. There is a fulfillment to your soul. You feel happy, you feel full. But when the call of the Lord and the call of those who are near to you begin to conflict with each other, that is the cross; and that is the time that you have to love the Lord more than anybody, any relationship.

Oftentimes, we cannot go well in the way of the Lord, and it is because our emotional life has not been dealt with. We are bound by human emotion, by human relationship, and it will shut up the life of Christ in us. That has to be cracked and broken. Does it mean to say, because of this, we will love our parents no more; we will love our brothers and sisters no more? No; but we will be delivered from that selfish love into that selfless love. We will be delivered from that natural love into that spiritual love; and we will love them even more and according to God. Family relationships, friendships, social relationships, all these that have something to do with our emotional life have to go to the cross.

Intellectual Life

When the Lord Jesus began to reveal that He must go to the cross and die and on the third day be raised from the dead, Peter, out of his good intention, laid hold of the Lord and said: "No, Lord, be kind to Yourself. Take care of Yourself; don't do that." And the Lord said, "You have offended Me because you mind the things of man and not the things of God" (see Matthew 16:21-23). Our mind, the intellectual life of our soul life has to be dealt with. Our mind, since the time of the Garden of Eden, has been deceived. Satan has built a stronghold in our minds, and how we need to be delivered from it. We think we are clever; we think we know everything; and the hardest thing to go to death is our opinion. We all have our opinion, and we think that our opinion is the best. We are terribly offended when people despise or neglect our opinion. We would rather die than to lose our opinion; but it has to go to death.

It does not mean God does not want us to have a good mind. As a matter of fact, God wants us to have a renewed mind; and with a renewed mind, then we can think much clearer. Therefore, if you want to think straight, you have to have a renewed mind; and then you can distinguish, you are able to see what is of God and what is not of God. God wants us to have a good mind, but you will not have it until you deliver that old, self-dominated mind to the cross.

Volitional Life

The same thing is true with our will. Some people are very strong-willed; you cannot move them. No reason can move them; no emotion can move them; no tears can move them. They are strong, like iron. However, it does not mean that God does not want us to have a will. He created that. As a matter of fact, a passive will is a very dangerous thing. But He wants a will that has been broken, a will that goes to the cross, a will that is able to will the will of God, not my will but Thy will be done.

Brothers and sisters, have you ever been dealt with in such a way? All the dealings before are somewhat outside of you; but unless your soul life is dealt with, the self, the I, the cross has not really implanted within you. You are still yourself. The Lord Jesus said, "Deny yourself, take up the cross and follow Me." What is denying self? How can we deny self? "I do not know you"; that is denying self. Peter denied, but he denied the wrong person. He should have denied himself, but he denied Christ. And that is what we have been doing all along. We know what denying is: "I do not know you. I have no obligation to follow you, to do your will." Denying self is a matter of willingness. When we are constrained by the love of Christ, then we are willing to deny ourselves. When we are shown the ugliness of ourselves, then we are willing to deny ourselves. If you see yourself as beautiful, you will never deny yourself. We need revelation. We need the love of Christ to constrain us, to make us willing to deny self. That is a matter of our will; and after we are willing to deny ourselves, then the Lord says, "Take up your cross and follow Me."

Brothers and sisters, you do not need to manufacture a cross for yourself, nor for other people. When you are willing to deny yourself, then the Holy Spirit will arrange crosses for you to take up and to bear. He will do it. He will arrange your circumstances, maybe through persons, through environment, through things, through events. He will arrange crosses for you to bear; and all these crosses are for one purpose: to put you on the cross. This is the only way for the rivers of living waters to be set free from you, and this is the only way that you come to know the authority of Christ over all the power of darkness.

Finally, the cross has to work in this matter of our natural strength. How often we try to serve God in our natural strength. We need to come to see it is not by might, nor by power but by His Spirit (Zechariah 4:6). This is the way of the cross; and it is not just a leap, a hop, but it is a step by step walking. We have to walk in the way of the cross because that way leads us to glory.

Shall we pray:

Dear Heavenly Father, Thou has shown us the way of the cross, where self is to be crucified. Lord, may Thy love constrain us that we may be willing to deny ourselves, to not trust ourselves, to abhor ourselves, to hate ourselves, to desire to be delivered from ourselves, that we may take up our cross and follow Thee. In the name of our Lord Jesus. Amen.

THE SPIRIT OF THE CROSS

Matthew 5:3-12 Blessed are the poor in spirit, for theirs is the kingdom of the heavens. Blessed they that mourn, for they shall be comforted. Blessed the meek, for they shall inherit the earth. Blessed they who hunger and thirst after righteousness, for they shall be filled. Blessed the merciful, for they shall find mercy. Blessed the pure in heart, for they shall see God. Blessed the peacemakers, for they shall be called sons of God. Blessed they who are persecuted on account of righteousness, for theirs is the kingdom of the heavens. Blessed are ye when they may reproach and persecute you, and say every wicked thing against you, lying, for my sake. Rejoice and exult, for your reward is great in the heavens; for thus have they persecuted the prophets who were before you.

The cross is not only a fact; it is not only dealings with us; it is not only a way that we can walk in, but the cross is a spirit. Unless that spirit of the cross comes upon us, we still have not entered into the significance of the cross. I read a book written by Gordon Watt, and the title of that book is The Meaning of the Cross; the subtitle is The Mold of the Cross. He said:

Our Lord Jesus Christ has just one mold for producing Christian character, and that is the cross. You and I cannot reach our goal except in the way in which He reached His goal, and the cross is the mold through which He puts each one who is to express Him here and reign with Him hereafter.

When we really know the cross, it will develop within us a character. We may call it the spirit of the cross. It will mark us out as people with that spirit. It becomes our very character. It is more than just an understanding, an appropriation, a dealing, or even a surrender. It becomes a life, a life style, a life principle. It becomes super-naturally natural to us, to all our actions and reactions. It marks us out as such a people. This is the spirit of the cross.

THE LAMB SPIRIT

Our Lord Jesus is called the Lamb slain from the foundation of the world. The Lamb of God has become His name, His title. From the foundation of the world, He is the Lamb slain. When He was on earth, He was called the Lamb of God, and as the Lamb of God, He went to the cross and there He died for us. After He was resurrected, He showed His wounds to Thomas; and after He was ascended, you find the Lamb slain in the midst of the throne. Our Lord Jesus has with Him that spirit of the Lamb, and that Lamb spirit is the spirit of the cross. Therefore, we who follow the Lamb need to be marked with the same spirit.

The epistle to the Galatian believers was a very difficult letter for the Apostle Paul to write, but he concluded that letter with these words: For the rest let no one trouble me, for I bear in my body the brands of the Lord Jesus (Galatians 6:17). There was the stigma of the Lord Jesus, the marks of the Lord Jesus in the life of the Apostle Paul. So the challenge to each one of us is this. We may have heard the word of the cross.

We may have experienced something of what the cross has done for us. We may know forgiveness, we may know separation, we may know deliverance and we may even know something of the victory of the cross. We may even walk, somehow, in the way of the cross and know something of the dealing with the selfhood, with the I, with the ego. But it is not just a dealing, a surrender, an experience here and there. The meaning of the cross is that we should be so molded by it that we will be characterized as the people of the cross. In other words, we have that Lamb spirit with us all the time. That is the meaning of the cross.

SEVEN WORDS SPOKEN ON THE CROSS

I think the best illustration of this is found in the seven words that our Lord Jesus spoke on the cross because we know words are really openings. Through these seven words that our Lord Jesus spoke on the cross, He poured forth His spirit to us; and by this, we can understand something of what the spirit of the cross is.

Spirit of Forgiveness

Of course, the first word that our Lord Jesus spoke on the cross is found in Luke 23:34:

And Jesus said, Father, forgive them, for they know not what they do.

He was being nailed to that cross and lifted up to die. The first word He uttered was: Father, forgive them for they know not what they do. Think of those circumstances. The men who had nailed Him to the cross surrounded the cross mocking Him, abusing Him, ridiculing Him, laughing at Him. In that kind of circumstance, suddenly, our Lord Jesus began to pray, Father, forgive them for they know not what they do. What a different spirit this is! There was no bitterness; there was only love.

Our Lord Jesus had every right to ask the Father for vengeance, that He would bring judgment upon the world. But instead of calling down revenge, He asked the Father to forgive. He could pray that prayer because there on the cross, He offered Himself as our substitute. God is just, and His justice has to be satisfied. God cannot forgive without His justice being satisfied. But our Lord Jesus, because He had offered Himself as the sin offering unto God, had the right to pray such a prayer, Father, forgive, and His prayer was answered.

What is the spirit of the cross? The spirit of the cross is forgiving love. Since the day our Lord Jesus was crucified, throughout church history, from the first Christian martyr, Stephen, down to our time, the last cry of the martyrs is always this: "Do not lay this sin upon them; forgive." The spirit of forgiveness is the very spirit of the cross.

Our greatest problem in the church today is the lack of the spirit of forgiveness. If we, as God's people, can keep a distance from each other, we can afford to be kind, gentle, and courteous. But God has thrown us together in such an intimate way; we work together, we serve together, we worship together. And because we are so close together, we begin to know each other better, and we begin to step on each other more. Therefore, it is inevitable that among God's people there will be plenty of opportunities for us to be offended. When such things happen, what is our spirit? Is our spirit that of calling for vengeance on our brothers and sisters? Or is it the time that we ask our Father to forgive? An unforgiving spirit hinders the blessing of the Lord, not only to the person himself or herself but it hinders God's blessing to the whole church. If we are followers of the Lamb, do we have such a spirit of forgiveness? No matter how much our brothers and sisters may offend us, and these offenses may be very real and we may be deeply hurt, if we look at the Lamb, if we know the spirit of the cross, there is nothing else we can do but to forgive.

You remember Peter. Peter was a very open person, straightforward, blunt, rough. One day, he came to the Lord and said, "My brother has offended me seven times, and I forgave him" (see Matthew 18:21). Now that was very difficult for Peter, so he felt that it was quite an accomplishment. But after forgiving his brother seven times, he felt the eighth time did not seem to be logical anymore. So he came to the Lord and said, "Will that be enough?" The Lord said, "I do not tell you seven times; it is seventy times seven" (see Matthew 18:22). This does not mean that you just count and multiply it; but it means that you just forget it. It has come to such a great amount that you just do not count them anymore; you do not remember them anymore. In other words, you forgive, forgive, forgive and forgive.

Sometimes, what the Lord says does not sink into our heart, and we think, "That is very unreasonable." So the Lord used a parable: A master had servants, and one of the servants owed him ten thousand talents. I do not know how he accumulated that amount, but he could never repay such a debt. He begged for mercy, and the master forgave him. When he left the presence of the master, he found a fellow servant who owed him a little, only a hundred denari, that is, the wages of a hundred days. And he said, "Pay; otherwise you go to jail." So he put him into jail. The master heard about it and said, "Now if I have forgiven you so much, should you not forgive your brother?" (see Matthew 18:24-33).

Brothers and sisters, is it not true, if we only realize how much we are forgiven, we will see we are those people who owe the Lord ten thousand talents? Even if we sell ourselves, our family, everything, we cannot repay it. It is beyond us; and yet our Lord Jesus, in His great mercy, asks the Father to forgive us. We are forgiven much, and should we not forgive those who offend us? This is the spirit of the cross. Are we a people marked by such a spirit?

We have such a wonderful memory. The good that others do for us, we forget altogether; but if our brother or sister would do to us, just one time, a tiny little thing that hurts us, we cannot forget; we cannot forgive. It is always there. Every time we see that brother or sister, there is something stirring within us. An unforgiving spirit, a bitter spirit is the reason why we do not grow properly in the Lord. That is the reason why we find so many problems in the church: brother and brother, sister and sister, brothers and sisters just cannot be of one mind, of one spirit, of one love. Remember this: The spirit of the cross is a spirit of forgiving.

Spirit of Grace

The second word that our Lord spoke on the cross is found in Luke 23:43:

And Jesus said to him, Verily I say to thee, Today shalt thou be with me in paradise.

Our Lord Jesus was crucified between two robbers. At the beginning, both of these robbers were wicked people, and even when they were crucified on the cross, they mocked and ridiculed the Lord Jesus. But something happened. When one of the robbers heard the prayer of our Lord Jesus to the Father, "Father, forgive them, for they know not what they do." I wonder if that prayer touched the heart of this robber. He was deeply touched and convicted. He knew he was dying because he deserved it but that Man was innocent; He had done nothing bad. Somehow, the Spirit of God opened his understanding, and what an understanding the Spirit of God gave to him at the very last of his life. He turned to the Lord and said: Remember me, Lord, when thou comest in thy kingdom (v.42). Now isn't that wonderful? Here was a man crucified; and yet the robber said, "Remember me when You come in Your kingdom." He believed that this Man who was being crucified was indeed the King. Even though He was crucified, yet His kingdom will come; and the robber asked that he be remembered. The Lord Jesus said: Verily, I say to thee, Today shalt thou be with me in paradise. Not in the future, you do not need to wait until the future, but today you shall be with Me in paradise. And we all know that paradise is the place where those who are accepted by God go. It is the resting place of the saints who fall asleep in the Lord. In other words, the Lord said, "You are forgiven; you are saved; you are redeemed."

The first word of our Lord Jesus was spoken to the Father; the second word He spoke to the sinner. The first word to the Father was, Forgive them; the second word to the sinner was, You are forgiven. What grace that is! This robber deserved nothing. He had done so much evil. Even in the eyes of society, he deserved to be put away; and he knew it. He deserved it. Yet, our Lord Jesus poured forth His grace to that robber and said, "Today shalt thou be with me in paradise."

What is the spirit of the cross? The spirit of the cross is the spirit of grace. Are we a people of grace? We have received grace upon grace. Grace is something freely given. It is not given to you because you are worthy, because you deserve it, because you have done something to earn it, to gain it, to win it; but grace is dependent upon the person who gives grace. Our Lord Jesus, on the cross, poured forth His grace upon that robber. We have received much grace. Should we not have the same character as our Lord Jesus had? Should we not be a people who are gracious, who give grace to other people? You know, brothers and sisters, we are very gracious with ourselves, but we are very strict with other people. We forgive ourselves, excuse ourselves, pardon ourselves, explain away; we are very gracious to ourselves. But when it come to other people, how do we deal with them? We feel that we have to deal with them according to what they deserve. We find that it is very difficult for us to be gracious to people. It is because we forget how much grace we have received.

The definition of grace, according to the original word, means that there is something beautiful, something pleasant in that person or that thing. And when you look at that thing or that person, it gives you a kind of peace, a comfortable sensation. It is because there in that thing or that person is something called grace. Grace, in the original language, not only means there is something beautiful there in that person but this something beautiful and good in that person is being transmitted, passed on to you freely. That is grace. But grace, in the original language, has a third meaning. It means that those who have received grace, in turn, become gracious.

Our Lord Jesus is full of grace. He is so beautiful; and thank God, we have received grace from Him, and grace upon grace. But has grace done its work in our lives? Has grace transformed us? Are we just receiving grace for ourselves, and yet it never transforms us? It never delivers us from our pettiness. It never delivers us from our selfhood, selfishness. It should transform us. Otherwise, we waste the grace of God. That is the spirit of the cross.

One Family

The third word our Lord Jesus said is found in John, chapter 19. When our Lord was crucified on the cross, some women were at the foot of the cross, and the mother of our Lord Jesus was there. Of all the disciples, only John was there with them.

Jesus therefore, seeing his mother, and the disciple standing by, whom he loved, says to his mother, Woman, behold thy son. Then he says unto His disciple, Behold thy mother. And from that hour the disciple took her to his own home. (John 19:26-27)

As a human being our Lord was perfect. You remember when He was a boy, twelve years old, He was conscious that God had called Him to be occupied with His Father's business. He stayed behind in the temple, and His parents came back after three days and found Him in the temple attending the Father's business. His mother said, "Now why, lad, did you do this to us?" And the Lord said, "Don't you know I must be occupied with My Father's business?" After He said that,

He went home with His parents and obeyed them.

Probably, one of the reasons why our Lord Jesus did not begin His ministry until He was thirty years old was because, humanly speaking, He was the first-born in that family. Seemingly, the father had passed away because Joseph was not mentioned anymore. So our Lord Jesus had a responsibility in that house and had to supply the needs for the family. He worked as a carpenter to support them, helping to bring up His brothers and sisters. This may have been the reason He did not come out to minister until He was thirty years old because, by then, His brothers and sisters had grown up, and they could take over some things. But our Lord Jesus, as a human being, fulfilled all the duties and obligations that a human being carries.

Sometimes, we become so spiritual that we become unnatural anymore. We are so spiritual that we forget our obligations and duties as a human being. But here you find, even to the very last, when our Lord Jesus was on the cross in great suffering, He was not thinking of Himself;

He was still thinking of His mother, and He wanted to provide for Her. So He said, "Mother, look at your son"; and to John, "Look at your mother." And John took Mary to his home and cared for her. Even to the very last, our Lord Jesus fulfilled all His duties and obligations as a human being.

Should we be less human? I think it is a gross mistake to think that to be spiritual, you have to be inhuman. I remember our dear brother Watchman Nee used to say, "First, be a human, and then you can be spiritual." If you are not human, you can never be spiritual.

However, what our Lord Jesus said in this third word, is much more than just this physical arrangement. When the Lord Jesus brought His mother and His disciple together to be one family, I think it speaks something to us: It is the cross that brings us together into one family. We belong to different families; we have many distinctions and backgrounds; but the cross takes away all these differences and brings those who are near and afar together into one. By the cross, He has made peace, not only between us and God but peace with one another. He has brought us together to be one family. Do we have this family feeling? Do we really see that we belong to each other? Or are we just taking care of ourselves? Our Lord Jesus said we need to love one another as He has loved us. We need to care for one another as He has cared for us because we belong to one another. We are of one family; and it is the cross that brings us into that family.

It is the cross that maintains us in the family. We are of the family of God, but sometimes, we feel we would like to leave that family. Sometimes, we feel we do not belong. Sometimes, we feel we want to go somewhere else. Maybe it is because what we want is not supplied. Maybe it is because we are hurt by our brothers and sisters. Maybe it is because there are things in our earthly background that are too strong for us, pulling us away from our brothers and sisters.

Through the cross of our Lord Jesus, all the distinctions, social distinctions, cultural distinctions, racial distinctions, national distinctions, are gone. There is neither Jew nor Gentile, neither circumcision nor uncircumcision, neither barbarian nor Scythian, neither bondman nor freeman (see Colossians 3:11) because the cross has done away with all these distinctions. We belong to one family, the family of God. We belong to one another. But sometimes, we try to bring our earthly distinctions into the church, and when we bring these things into the church, it divides the family. But look at the cross, what our Lord Jesus has done for us, what suffering He has gone through, what it has cost Him in order to bring us together into one family. Do you not think we need to allow the cross to work in our lives to cross out all these distinctions and find that, in Christ, we are one family? That is the spirit of the cross.

The Spirit of Sacrifice

Our Lord Jesus was on the cross from approximately nine o'clock in the morning until twelve o'clock. During those three hours, He was surrounded by the people mocking Him, laughing at Him. And not only that, but in the unseen world, during those three hours, He was surrounded by the powers of darkness attacking Him. He suffered. But then at twelve o'clock, the whole thing changed. The sun was darkened, and nobody could see Him anymore. Hanging there alone, He cried out, My God, my God, why hast thou forsaken me? (Matthew 27:46). It was at that time God accepted Him as the offering for sin; and because of that, according to Isaiah 53:10, God, Himself, crushed Him; God, Himself, bruised Him. He was made a sin offering for the world.

Our Lord Jesus was with the Father even before time, in eternity. The communion between the Father and Him was so sweet; there was no shadow; there was no shade. Even when He was on earth, He always pleased the Father: This is my beloved Son, in whom I have found my delight (Matthew 3:17). Even from eternity, through time, His communion with the Father was never for a second interrupted. There was sweet communion, and it was this that gave Him strength to endure all the ridicule, all the sufferings from the seen and the unseen foes; but there, at that time, the Father left Him. For three hours, He literally tasted hell; He literally tasted, for us, the second death.

Brothers and sisters, what is hell? What is second death? It is separation from the living God; and there our Lord Jesus was separated from the living God. He could not cry out, "Father," He could only say, "My God, My God" because He took our stand as a man; and for man, He died. It was the supreme sacrifice. There He willingly sacrificed Himself. We can never understand how much He sacrificed for us. This is the spirit of the cross, and this spirit must characterize us.

It is true, we have no part in that atoning work of our Lord Jesus. He trod the wine press alone, for us. He who knew no sin was made sin for us that we might be made the righteousness of God (see II Corinthians 5:21). He is alone there. We have no part in that atoning work. We can only receive forgiveness from it. But we are called to have fellowship with His sufferings. There is a part of His sufferings that we are called to have fellowship with; and throughout the centuries, there have been people who know that fellowship. Think of Moses. When the children of Israel worshipped the golden calf and God wanted to wipe out that nation and make Moses a nation and bless him, how Moses pleaded before God: "Lord, forgive them. If not, blot out my name from the book that you have written" (see Exodus 32:32). In other words, he was willing to be blotted out of the book of life in order to save this rebellious people. That is the spirit of the cross.

In the New Testament we have another example, Paul.

For I have wished, I myself, to be a curse from the Christ for my brethren, my kinsmen, according to flesh. (Romans 9:3)

His love for his kinsmen, his brethren, was so great that he was willing to be a curse if these could be blessed. Now that is the spirit of the cross.

Brothers and sisters, are we marked by that spirit? Have we been molded by that spirit? The Lord Jesus said: "Love one another. As I have laid down My life for you, lay down your life for your brethren" (see I John 3:16). Is any sacrifice for our brothers and sisters too great for us? Are we willing to lay down our life for others? What a different spirit we have. We want our brothers and sisters to lay down their lives for us, but for us to lay down our life for them is out of the question. We do not have the spirit of the cross. How much has the cross molded us? Are we still the same, as if we know nothing about the cross? If we know something of the cross, to sacrifice ourselves to complete our brothers and sisters is nothing hard.

Spirit of Absolute Trust in God

Towards the end of that six hours on the cross, we find the fifth word in John 19:28:

After this, Jesus, knowing that all things were now finished, that the scripture might be fulfilled, says, I thirst. There was a vessel therefore there full of vinegar, and having filled a sponge with vinegar, and putting hyssop round it, they put it up to his mouth.

When our Lord Jesus cried out, My God, my God, why hast thou forsaken me? it was a spiritual cry, a cry of spiritual sufferings. In other words, so far as the spirit of our Lord Jesus was concerned, He suffered to the fullest extent because His spirit was separated from God the Spirit. So that intense suffering in His spirit caused Him to cry out, My God, my God, why hast thou forsaken me? But He cried out again: I thirst. This was a cry due to His physical suffering. It was a fulfillment of Psalm 69, where it says:

Yea, they gave me gall for my food, and in my thirst they gave me vinegar to drink. (v.21)

Through that almost six hours on the cross, our Lord Jesus never thought of His physical sufferings. If you were crucified on the cross, what else could you think about? Tremendous sufferings. But during those six hours, He never had a thought of Himself. He thought of the people who crucified Him; He thought of the robber by His side; He thought of His mother and the disciple; He never thought of Himself. Only at the very end did He become conscious of His extreme sufferings, excruciating sufferings, physically. Do not think that our Lord Jesus, because He was God, did not suffer when He was crucified. He suffered tremendously. In Psalm 22, the Psalmist, in that prophetic foresight, saw what our Lord Jesus went through on the cross, how His life was poured out like water, how His bones were all out of joint, how His heart was melted like wax, and how He was so thirsty that His tongue cleaved to His upper palate. The blood of our Lord Jesus had been drained from His whole body; and when that happens, of course, you are thirsty. He said, I thirst.

But I believe there was something more. It is said: "..that the Scripture might be fulfilled, says, I thirst." I believe there was something more when He said, I thirst. We read in Psalm 42:

As the hart panteth after the water brooks, so panteth my soul after thee, O God. My soul thirsteth for God, for the living God: when shall I come and appear before God? (v.1-2)

I believe when our Lord Jesus said, "I thirst," it was more than just a physical thirst. He, being a sin offering on the cross, separated from God, and the work of redemption being almost done, at the very last, He said: "I thirst. No matter what

I have gone through, no matter that God had hidden His face from Me, no matter that God crushed Me, I still thirst for Him." There is such absolute trust, confidence in God.

Brothers and sisters, we remember Job once said: Behold, if He slay me, yet would I trust in him (Job 13:15). Our Lord Jesus was not offended by God. If anyone could be offended by God, He should be because He had every reason to see the smiling face of the Father; but God turned His face from Him. Yet our Lord was not offended. He said, I thirst. As the hart panteth after the water brooks, so my soul panteth after thee. My soul thirsteth for the living God.

Dear brothers and sisters, how easily we are offended. Even John the Baptist was almost offended because the Lord did not do what he expected Him to do. The Lord seemed to neglect him. The Lord did good to many people but it was as if He had forgotten him. He was almost offended; but the Lord said, "Blessed are those who are not offended by Me" (see Matthew 11:6). Is it not true that in your Christian walk, sometimes, the Lord does not do what you expect Him to do? You may have every right to expect Him to do because you have His word, but it is as if He goes back on His word. He allows things to happen, and you cannot explain it; and there is no way out. It looks like death, the end. Are you offended? Do you at that point cry out and say: "I thirst after You. No matter what You did to me, I believe in You; I trust in You. You are trustworthy; I know it." That is the spirit of the cross. May we be a people marked as such.

Spirit of Victory

The sixth word is found in John 19:30:

When therefore Jesus had received the vinegar, he said, It is finished.

In the other gospels, we find: He shouted out with a loud shout, (It is finished) (Matthew 27:50, Mark 15:37, Luke 23:46). In other words, He gathered up the last of His remaining strength. The voice of a person who is dying will be very low because there is no strength anymore, but here our Lord Jesus gathered up the remainder of His strength, and He shouted out, "It is finished." It was a shout of victory; it was not defeat. Outwardly, it looked like a defeat; but actually, it was a victory. It is finished. The work of redemption is done. The mission is accomplished. What a shout of victory it was. When He shouted that shout, an amazing thing happened. In the temple in the city of Jerusalem, the veil was rent from top to bottom. The way to the holiest was opened for us to enter.

Brothers and sisters, the spirit of the cross is not a spirit of defeat. Oftentimes, people misunderstand, and when they talk about the cross, it gives them a feeling of negativeness, a feeling of defeat. "Oh, I suffer; oh, I die." That kind of negative feeling is not the spirit of the cross. The spirit of the cross is the cry of victory. Oftentimes, people say: "Well, I'm bearing the cross. Look at me, how I bear the cross, how I suffer." That is no cross. If you are really bearing the cross, you find strength in the cross of Christ, you find rest and you can shout the victory. By the cross, you conquer. That is the spirit of the cross.

Spirit of Perfect Faith

The seventh word is found in Luke 23:46:

And Jesus, having cried with a loud voice, said, Father, into thy hands I commit my spirit.

This was a fulfillment of Psalm 31:5: Into thy hand I commit my spirit: thou hast redeemed me, Jehovah, thou God of truth.

During that three hours, the work of redemption was done; and He said, "It is finished." After that work was done, His relation with His Father was restored, so He said, "Father." That was His last word, Father. That relationship was restored, and He said, Into Thy hands I commit My spirit. No one took away the life of our Lord Jesus. You remember He said: "No one takes My life away. I lay it down and I take it up" (see John 10:17-18). It was not those people who crucified Him who took away His life; He dismissed His own life. He said, Father, into thy hands I commit My spirit. He laid His life down for us, and He committed His spirit to the Father, knowing that His Father would raise Him from the dead. That is perfect faith. And sure enough, the Father raised Him from the dead to prove that He is the Son of God. He could trust Himself completely to the Father, knowing that the Father would do all things right. The spirit of the cross is the spirit of perfect faith. If we know the cross, brothers and sisters, the cross will give us that faith. Because we try to escape from the cross, we miss the opportunity of believing; but if we take up the cross, faith will be given to us. We can believe that God does all things well. This is the spirit of the cross.

If we know the cross, then the cross will not be just something external, outside of us, a doctrine, a teaching for us to talk about. If we really know the cross, it is not just some dealings here and there, which of course we need; but the cross will be planted within our souls, and it will reshape us, mold us so that we may have the Lamb spirit within us. We become the people of the cross, and that is what God is doing.

I read the Beatitudes at the beginning, and there you find these are the people blessed by God. These are the sons of the kingdom of the heavens. They are the people of the cross. They are poor in spirit because the cross has worked in their life. They are those who mourn because the cross has so worked in them, they are in continuous repentance with a contrite spirit before God. They are the meek, that is selfless, because the cross has crossed out their self. They hunger and thirst after righteousness; they are thirsty after God. They are meek; they are lowly; they are merciful because they know mercy. They are pure in heart; they have nothing in their heart but God. They are the peacemakers because they know what peace is. And for the sake of Christ, they are being persecuted; yet they rejoice. These are the people of the cross. So our problem is: Do we know the cross? Is there any scar, any wound in our lives? Do we have the marks of the Lord Jesus in our body? May the Lord have mercy upon us.

Shall we pray:

Dear Heavenly Father, we can only come to Thee and say, "May Thy cross be so implanted in us that it will transform us, fashion us, mold us according to Thy beloved Son, the Lamb of God." We ask in Jesus' name. Amen.

THE GLORY OF THE CROSS

Hebrews 12:1-2 Let us also therefore, having so great a cloud of witnesses surrounding us, laying aside every weight, and sin which so easily entangles us, run with endurance the race that lies before us, looking steadfastly on Jesus the leader and completer of faith: who, in view of the joy lying before him, endured the cross, having despised the shame, and is set down at the right hand of the throne of God.

Oftentimes, when we mention the word cross, we are afraid. We know that the cross means death, and we do not want to die. But we have to know that there is another side, the glory of the cross. Think of our Lord Jesus. In Hebrews 12, we are told for the joy that is set before Him, He endured the cross. The reason why our Lord Jesus was able to endure the cross, and what a cross it was, was because of the joy set before Him. After He had endured the cross, despising the shame, God set Him at the right hand of the throne.

DEATH AND RESURRECTION

Dr. Mabie said: "In the thought of Scripture, the reconciling death and resurrection have always been taken together. They are inseparable parts of a real unity, twin parts of one fact." In other words, when we talk about the cross, we have to remember that death and resurrection are joined together in that cross. They are twin parts of one fact. In teaching and in experience of the cross, we have to strike that balance. If we overemphasize the death aspect of the cross and neglect the life aspect of the cross, the teaching will become very heavy, dark, gloomy, oppressive, and negative. Or if we overemphasize the life aspect of the cross and neglect the death side of it, we become very superficial in our teaching because, without death, there can be no resurrection.

So far as our Christian experience goes, it is the same. Some people stress so much the death side, dead to sin, dead to the world, dead to self, dead to everything, they are dead. There is no life, no livingness, no freshness; it is all inactivity, passivity, paralysis. This is no

Christian life. On the other hand, there are people who stress so much the life side, they try to avoid everything on the death side because they think that is very unpleasant. The result is what they consider as spiritual life, actually, is a pretension, a falsehood, a substitute. They substitute their natural life for spiritual life because they do not know death.

Brother Sparks mentioned this: "Of course, it is understood that the phrase the cross does not merely mean crucifixion of Christ but the death, the burial, the resurrection, and ascension to the throne, and the sovereign relationship rests now in Christ there for us. All is by way of the cross. We never see the throne apart from the Lamb in the midst thereof, as though it had been slain. Everything is gathered up in the phrase Jesus Christ and Him crucified. And when the cross is mentioned, Christ crucified, with all that that implies, is meant." Therefore, when we are talking about the cross, we have to remember that it does not mean only the death side. We need the death side; but whenever we talk about the cross, we have to remember there is the resurrection side. Death and life, Calvary and resurrection, you cannot separate them because this is what the cross really is.

We thank the Lord that our Lord Jesus was crucified on the cross. He was buried; but on the third day, He was raised from the dead. You remember the apostle said in I Corinthians 15, if Christ has not been raised from the dead, then our faith is in vain, and we are still in sin. But thank God, our Lord Jesus not only died for us and was buried for us but He was raised from the dead for us. He was the first fruit raised; and in Him, we are all made alive, life out of death.

We have to remember that the life we originally have which we received from our parents, our forefathers, that Adamic life, has been poisoned. It is corrupted, it is sinful and selfish; it cannot be reformed nor improved; and that life deserves nothing but death. But there is a life that can go into death and come out, and this is the life that our Lord Jesus has offered to us.

What is life? We need to know what life really is. This soul life of ours is no life at all because this natural life, one day, will die. There is not only the first death but there is the second death, eternal death. That is the reason why our Lord Jesus came into this world to be a Man. He went into death in order to rob the one who had the power of death, in order to bring death to death. Everybody who goes into death will never be able to come out; but our Lord Jesus, the very source of life, was able to enter into death, rob death of its power, and destroy death. He came out of death; and in coming out, He gave His life to those who believe in Him. The cross is the place where life is released. The cross is the place where death happened; but it is death to the old life; it is life to the new life.

Baptism

Are you ignorant that we, as many as have been baptised unto Christ Jesus, have been baptised unto his death? We have been buried therefore with him by baptism unto death, in order that, even as Christ has been raised up from among the dead by the glory of the Father, so we also should walk in newness of life. For if we are become identified with him in the likeness of his death, so also we shall be of his resurrection. (Romans 6:3-5)

When we are baptized we go into the water, and as we go into the water, it is identification with the likeness of the death of our Lord Jesus. His death was an all-inclusive death because sin, the world, the enemy, self, Adam, all these, were put to death. And when we are baptized, the moment we step into the water, we become identified with the likeness of His death. When we are underneath the water, we are buried with Him; and when we come out of the water, we become identified with the likeness of His resurrection. In other words, when we are baptized, we act out our faith. We believe that we are dead in Christ and with Him; we believe we are buried with Him; and we believe we have been raised with Him. So we act out our faith by baptism. It tells us that if we are identified with His death and die to sin, to the world and to our Adamic life, our selfhood, then by faith we know that we are also identified with Him in His resurrection. Now we live unto God; and by this new life, we can walk and serve God in newness of life. This is most basic and most important.

Brothers and sisters, it is very sad that many of God's people still do not see this. They believe in the Lord Jesus, they know their sins are forgiven, and yet, somehow, they try to live their Christian life by the old life in them; and because of that, there is no life at all. The more you try to be like a Christian, the less you become a Christian. You find it is a total failure because there is no one who can live a Christian life but Christ; and thank God, on the cross, He has released that life. We have that life in us, and all we need to do is let that life be set free. Oftentimes, it is not that we do not have that resurrection life in us but it is bound up, locked up by our old life. That is why death is so important. We need to see the death side of the cross, and the reason for that is not negative. It is positive because it is to release the resurrection life in us.

TRANSFORMATION

The cross is the secret of transformation. There on the cross, God is doing the work of transforming us. It is almost like an ugly caterpillar that goes through a metamorphosis.

When that process is completed, out comes a beautiful butterfly. It is no longer earthbound; it is heavenbound. Brothers and sisters, this is what the cross is doing for us. The cross is to put to death our soul life, that ugly caterpillar, and to transform us into that beautiful butterfly, in resurrection life that goes heavenward.

We think of Jacob. No doubt, Jacob suffered a great deal because of what he was. But thank God, through all the sufferings and the dealings of the cross in his life, God was able to transform him from Jacob to Israel. Do you know God is doing the same thing with us? How we need the cross daily to put us to death that daily Christ may be released in us. That is the glory of the cross.

FRUITFULNESS

Furthermore, the glory of the cross is in fruitfulness. Our Lord Jesus said, "You have not chosen Me, but I have chosen you that you may go and bear much fruit" (see John 15:16). If we bear fruit, we will be His disciples, and we will glorify the Father. But how can we bear fruit? In John 12:24, the Lord said, "Verily, verily, I say unto you, Except the grain of wheat falling into the ground die, it abides alone." In other words, it will not bear fruit. "But if it die, it bears much fruit."

Dr. Andrew Murray once said, "No one knows what fruit is until he has learned to die to all that is merely human." I do not know if you agree with him. You may think, surely, we can bear fruit; surely, we can do a lot for God. But this statement is so spiritually true: "No one knows what fruit is until he has learned to die to all that is merely human.

What is fruit? Fruit is the result of abundant life. Fruit is effortless. When a tree is bearing fruit, it is not even conscious that it is bearing fruit. It is because there is such an abundance of life within that it produces fruit. We may see an artificial orange tree with oranges on it; but they are tied to the tree. Isn't that what we have been doing? We substitute fruit with work. When you are doing something, of course, you are conscious of it. You have put lots of effort into it; and if there is some result, not only do you want people to appreciate it, you are the first one who appreciates it. You are full of self-consciousness. But that is work. That is something we do by ourselves with our cleverness, with our plans, with our will power, with our natural energy. They are not fruits; they are imitation. They may look good in this world, but they do not satisfy the hungry hearts, neither God's nor man's.

Gordon Watt said: "How difficult it is to die to dependence on our own intellect or to pride in our abilities or to our reputation or to our natural desire for success or to self-made plans; but fruit comes when we are willing that all these should go to the cross while Christ becomes everything and we depend entirely on the Holy Spirit for every word we speak, every work we do, and every path of life we take." It is very hard to die to our dependence on our own intellect. It is very hard to die to our pride in our abilities; we think we are able. It is very difficult to die to our reputation; we want to make a reputation and keep it. It is very difficult to die to the desire for success; we want to produce something that will glorify us. It is very difficult to die to our plans; we have all our plans laid out, even in so-called "service to God." But unless we are willing to die to all these, we can produce no fruit because the fruit is the fruit of the Spirit. It is the abundant life of Christ; and it is only the Holy Spirit who is able to release that abundant life and produce fruit that will be a pleasure to God and to man. And if you are bearing fruit, you do not need to make a great noise, you do not need to sound a trumpet. Quietly, silently, the fruit is there. The glory of the cross is fruit bearing. The more we know the cross, the more fruit will come forth.

MINISTRY

The glory of the cross is ministry. We all want ministry. We want to serve; we want to be useful to God. And I believe that this is right because we are saved to serve. But what is true ministry? How does spiritual ministry come into being?

For we do not preach ourselves, but Christ Jesus Lord, and ourselves your bondmen for Jesus' sake. Because it is the God who spoke that out of darkness light should shine who has shone in our hearts for the shining forth of the knowledge of the glory of God in the face of Jesus Christ. But we have this treasure in earthen vessels. (II Corinthians 4:5-7)

We are all earthen vessels, but we think we are alabaster flasks. We are earthen vessels, nothing. Only God will do that because man will never put a treasure in an earthen vessel. Only God will put a treasure in an earthen vessel. And the treasure, of course, is our Lord Jesus; there is none else.

Thank God, there is that treasure in the earthen vessel. There is that brilliancy, radiancy, that glory of life within us; but we are earthen vessels, opaque. We shut in, imprison the brilliancy, the light of the knowledge of God in Jesus Christ within us, and for us to minister Christ to people, this earthen vessel has to be broken. Oftentimes, we minister by the power of the earthen vessel, and some earthen vessels are quite ornate. They have cleverness, a dynamic personality, a strong will, full of energy, full of thoughts; and they try to minister by these things. With our clever mind, we analyze the Bible; with our eloquence, we try to persuade people; with our dynamic personality, we overwhelm people; but is this ministry? Ministry is the imparting of Christ; it is ministering Christ to people. Such ministry is only possible through the cross because it is the cross that breaks the earthen vessel. In II Corinthians 4, Paul mentioned how, in every way, he was afflicted but not straitened. He was literally sur-rounded, as if there were no way to go; but there is always a way up. He said we see no apparent issue, but our way is not entirely shut up. One translation says, "We are at our wit's end but not at our life's end." And how often this happens. He said we are persecuted, but not abandoned; cast down, but not destroyed. Phillip's translation says, Knocked down but not knocked out (II Corinthians 4:9).

This is the experience of the ministers of God's Word. Unless you have gone through this breaking of the outward man, the life, the brilliancy, the radiancy of Christ Jesus within you is just imprisoned. There is only one way that the spirit life is released, and that is through the cracking and the breaking of the earthen vessel, our soul life, and that is ministry. The Apostle Paul said, "I bear in my body the dying of

Jesus that the life of Jesus might be in you" (see II Corinthians 4:10). Without the cross, there is no ministry. Unfortunately, today we have so much so-called "ministry" without the cross. May the Lord help us see that the glory of the cross is ministry. If you have to go through the cross in order that you may minister to your brothers and sisters, are you willing to go through? It is worth it.

THE THRONE

The glory of the cross is the throne. Think of how our Lord Jesus walked the way of the cross. He emptied Himself; He took the form of a slave, even the fashion of a man; and being in the likeness of man, He humbled Himself; and He went into death, even the death of the cross. But God has highly exalted Him and has given Him a name that is above every name, and to that name every knee shall bow, every tongue confess that Jesus is Lord. The cross is the way to the throne; and if this is true with our Lord Jesus, it is true with us. In II Timothy 2, we are told if we endure with Him, we shall reign with Him. There is no other way.

The cross is something that you can escape; and that is the reason why the Lord said, "Take up your cross." In other words, if you decide not to take it up, you are able to do that. But today, if you do not deny yourself, take up the cross and follow the Lord, you may gain your life now, for a time, satisfaction and fulfillment in your soul life, but you will lose the throne. And what God has destined us for is the throne.

THE CHURCH

The glory of the cross is the church. Our Lord Jesus said, "I will build My church upon this rock, and the gates of Hades shall not prevail against it" (see Matthew 16:18). Immediately following that, He told His disciples how He had to go to Jerusalem and to die; but on the third day, He would be raised from the dead. In other words, for the church to come into being, Christ had to go to the cross. There on the cross, that soldier thrust a spear into His side and drew out from His side blood and water. John testified and said he saw it, and what he saw was real, was true; and he repeated it (see John 19:34-37). It is not just for this physical phenomenon; it is because there is that reality there. Out of the pierced side of our Lord Jesus came blood and water; and with this, He builds His church. It is like when God put Adam to sleep, opened his side, and took out a rib; and with that rib, He built a woman. Adam's sleep was a painless sleep because that was before sin entered into the world; but the sleep of our Lord Jesus on the cross was most painful because of sin. Out of His side came blood to atone our sins and water as life to give us life; and with that life, we will be built up together into His church.

In Ephesians 5, it is said:

He loved the church and gave Himself for it, in order that He might sanctify it, purifying it by the washing of water by the word, that He may present to Himself a glorious church without spot or wrinkle or any of such sort, holy and without blemish (vv.25-27).

Not only did our Lord Jesus use His blood and His life to build the church, but He is continuously purifying the church with the water by the word. He uses His word and His life working together to sanctify the church, to make it a glorious church without spot or wrinkle, suitable for Himself.

The church is found on the foundation of the cross of Christ; and the church, even today, is being built by the cross. If we, as living stones, do not accept the cross in our lives, we will not fit in with one another. We all have our corners. Our strength is that corner that needs to be knocked off. But are we willing to be sawed, chiseled, smoothed, reduced? If not, no stone will fit with another stone. When the temple of Solomon was built, it was said that there was no sound of iron because all the stones were cut, chiseled and smoothed according to measure, according to plan. Every stone was cut to fit with one another and had a number on it. All they needed to do was transport the stones to Mount Moriah where they put them one on another, without the sound of iron. It was all done in secret, in darkness, in the quarry. Brothers and sisters, if we do not allow the cross to work in our lives to knock off our corners, what will happen? In the open, when we try to build up with one another there will be lots of sound of iron; and that is what is happening. We rub against each other; we stick against each other. There is lots of fire and noise because, in secret, we fail to accept the working of the cross in our lives.

God has called us to be a habitation for Him. We are to be built up together. You are not called to be a monument standing by yourself. You are called to be a stone fit in with another stone, and in order to be fit, you have to be cut. Probably, what you consider as your strength, as your beauty is the very thing that needs to be knocked off. Now are you willing to do that for the sake of the building of God's house? The cross is the only way, but when the cross has done its work, oh, what a beautiful, glorious temple of God is built! The cross gives us the church. So we often say, "If you preach the church, you get the cross; if you preach the cross, you get the church." If you talk too much about the church, you get the cross because that is the way the church is to be built. Let us talk about the cross, and the church will come out.

ACCOMPLISHMENT OF THE ETERNAL PURPOSE

Finally, the glory of the cross is the accomplishment of the eternal purpose of God. We mentioned at the very beginning that this universe has two aspects. If you look at the aspect of the eternal purpose of God, it is centered upon the Person of our Lord Jesus; but if you look at the incursion of sin and its effects, then the universe is Redempto-centric.

We also say that the cross is God's means to God's end. What is God's end? What is His eternal purpose? His eternal purpose is that His Son may have the first place in all things. His eternal purpose is to sum up all things in Christ Jesus. His eternal purpose is that Christ may be all and in all. That is God's eternal purpose. But how can that eternal purpose be fulfilled? It can only be fulfilled by the way of the cross. The cross is the only means to God's eternal end. By the working of the cross of our Lord Jesus, by our taking up our cross and following Him, the result is all that is not of Christ will be taken away and all that is of Christ will be established until, one day, we will see the holy city, new

Jerusalem. God said: "It is done; I have made all things new. Old things have all passed away, sin, the world, natural life, self, the enemy, the power of darkness. The old creation has passed away, and all is new creation in Christ Jesus" (see Revelation 21). God's end is reached through God's means. Christ becomes all and in all after the cross has done its work. So may the Lord help us.

Shall we pray:

Dear Heavenly Father, we worship Thee. We worship Thee because the word of the cross to those who perish is foolishness but to us who believe, who are saved, it is the power of God. Oh, how we praise and thank Thee for the cross of Christ Jesus. We embrace it; we love it. We are willing to take up our cross and follow Thee that Thy purpose concerning thy beloved Son might be fulfilled, that Thou will have a bride for Thy beloved Son to His glory. In the name of our Lord Jesus. Amen.

Other Books Printed By
Christian Testimony Ministry

Speaker	Title
Dana Congdon	Marriage, Singleness, and the Will of God
	Recovery & Restoration
	The Holy Spirit
	Hebrews
A.J. Flack	Tent of His Splendour
Stephen Kaung	Acts
	Be Ye Therefore Perfect
	Called Out Unto Christ
	Called to the Fellowship of God's Son
	Divine Life and Order
	For Me to Live is Christ
	Glorious Liberty of the Children of God
	God's Purpose for the Family
	I Will Build My Church
	Meditations on the Kingdom
	Recovery
	Spiritual Exercise
	Spiritual Life (II Corinthians Series)
	Teach Us to Pray
	The Cross
	The Fulness of Christ—In the Book of Revelation
	The Headship of Christ
	The Kingdom and the Church
	The Kingdom of God
	The Last Call to the Churches, the Call to Overcome
	The Life of Our Lord Jesus
	The Life of the Church, the Body of Christ
	The Lord's Table
	Two Guideposts for Inheriting the Kingdom
	Vision of Christ (Revelation)
	Who Are We?

www.ingramcontent.com/pod-product-compliance
Lightning Source LLC
Chambersburg PA
CBHW060527030426
42337CB00015B/2007